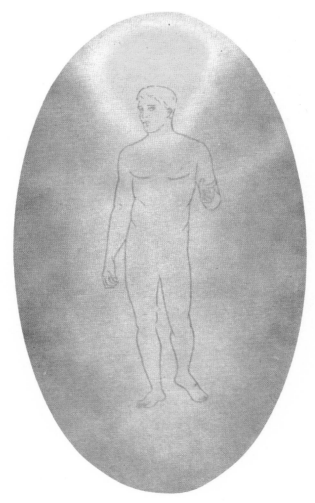

Plate I. The Astral Body of the Developed Man

The
Riddle
of
Life

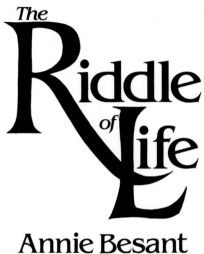

The Riddle of Life

Annie Besant

THE THEOSOPHICAL PUBLISHING HOUSE
Wheaton, IL U.S.A. / Madras, India / London, England

Contents

Illustrations

Annie Besant had after many explorations found her path and come to see the universe and herself in their real perspective.

George Bernard Shaw

Foreword

A few times in a century a figure arises who has spiritual depth and vision as well as outstanding qualities of leadership. Annie Besant was such a person. Second president of the Theosophical Society, she was a student of Helena P. Blavatsky, one of the founders of the Society. She studied ancient scriptures of Eastern religions and developed her own clairvoyant powers to seek out truth firsthand. She reached thousands through her oratory in which she expressed the truths of theosophy with simplicity, force, and beauty.

The theosophical ideas which Mrs. Besant spread so effectively in her day are even more widespread now near the end of the twentieth century. Innumerable books and groups teach aspects of these truths. Yet few have the balanced, overall perspective of a mind like hers which was permeated with the essence of the teaching. Few can compare with her clarity which never stoops to oversimplification. Therefore, the reprinting of her little classic, *The Riddle of Life,* seems timely and needed. This is an overview of the theosophical philosophy, giving the highlights but with enough detail to indicate the intricacies. It will serve as an introduction to newcomers in this area of thought and will also add something new and enriching to those already familiar with the concepts.

This material first appeared in serial form in *The Theosophist* under the title "Elementary Theosophy." It was then published as a small book in answer to the demand for clear statements of theosophy's answers to the riddle of life. The only alterations to Mrs. Besant's original words are minor deletions or revisions of a few phrases or sentences which are dated and no longer pertinent. The eloquence of her style with its Victorian expressions has been preserved.

SHIRLEY NICHOLSON,
Editor

I

The Meaning of Theosophy

*T*he word *Theosophy* is now on the lips of many, and as M. Jourdain spoke prose without knowing it, so many are Theosophists who do not realise it. For Theosophy is Divine Wisdom, and that Wisdom is the Light which lighteth every man who cometh into the world. It belongs to none exclusively; it belongs to each inclusively; the power to receive it is the right to possess it; the fact of possession makes the duty of sharing. Every religion, every philosophy, every science, every activity, draws what it has of truth and beauty from the Divine Wisdom, but cannot claim it as its own against others. Theosophy does not belong to the Theosophical Society; the Theosophical Society belongs to Theosophy.

What is the essence of Theosophy? It is the fact that man, being himself divine, can know the Divinity whose life he shares.* As an inevitable corollary to this supreme truth comes the fact of the Brotherhood of Man. The divine Life is the spirit in everything that exists, from the atom to the archangel; the grain of dust could not be were God absent from it; the loftiest seraph is but a spark from the eternal Fire which is God. Sharers in one Life, all form one Brotherhood. The immanence of God, the solidarity of Man, such are the basic truths of Theosophy.

Its secondary teachings are those which are the common teachings of all religions, living or dead: the Unity of God; the triplicity of His nature; the descent of Spirit into matter, and hence the hierarchies of intelligences, whereof humanity is one; the growth of humanity by the unfoldment of consciousness and the evolution of bodies, *i.e.,* reincarnation; the progress of this growth under inviolable law, the law of causality, *i.e.,* karma; the environment to this growth, the three worlds, physical, astral, and mental, or earth, the intermediate world, and heaven; the existence of divine Teachers, superhuman men.

All religions teach or have taught these, though from time to time one or another of these teachings may temporarily fall into the background; ever they

---

*The word *man* is used in this book to denote humanity, both women and men.

reappear—as the doctrine of reincarnation fell out of ecclesiastical Christianity but is now returning to it, was submerged but is again emerging.

It is the mission of the Theosophical Society as a whole to spread these truths in every land, though no individual member is bound to accept any one of them; every member is left absolutely free, to study as he pleases, to accept or to reject; but if the Society, as a collectivity, ceased to accept and to spread them, it would also cease to exist.

This unity of teachings among the world religions is due to the fact that they are all founded by members of the Brotherhood of divine Teachers, the custodian of the Divine Wisdom, of Theosophy. From this Brotherhood come out, from time to time, the Founders of new religions, who ever bring with them the same teachings, but shape the form of those teachings to suit the conditions of the time, such as the intellectual stage of the people to whom They come, their type, their needs, their capacities. The essentials are ever the same; the non-essentials vary. This identity is shown in the symbols which appear in all faiths, for symbols form the common language of religions. The circle, the triangle, the cross, the eye, the sun, the star, with many another, ever bear their silent testimony to the fundamental unity of the religions of the world. Understanding this, the Theosophical Society serves every religion within its own domain, and draws them together into a Brotherhood.

In morals, Theosophy builds its teachings on the Unity, seeing in each form the expression of a common Life, and therefore the fact that what injures one injures all. To do evil, *i.e.,* to throw poison into the life-blood of humanity, is a crime against the Unity. Theosophy has no code of morals, being itself the embodiment of the highest morality; it presents to its students the highest moral teachings of all religions, gathering the most fragrant blossoms from the gardens of the world's faiths. Its Society has no code, for any code that could be generally imposed would be at the average low level of the day, and the Society seeks to raise its members above the ordinary level by ever presenting to them the highest ideals, and infusing into them the loftiest aspirations. It seeks to evolve the inner law, not to impose an outer. Its method with its least evolved members is not expulsion, but reformation.

The embodiment of the Divine Wisdom in an organisation gives a nucleus from which its life-forces may radiate. A new and strong link is thus made between the spiritual and the material worlds; it is in very truth a Sacrament, "the outward and visible sign of an inward and spiritual grace," a witness of the Life of God in Man.

II

The Solar System

A Solar System is a group of worlds circling round a central Sun, from which they draw light, life and energy. On this all Theosophists and non-Theosophists are agreed. But the Theosophist sees much more than this in a Solar System. It is to him a vast Field of Evolution, presided over by a divine Lord, who has created its matter out of the ether Space, permeating this matter with His Life, organizing it into His Body, and from His Heart, the Sun, pouring out the energy which circulates through the System as its life-blood—life-blood which returns to the Heart when its nutrient properties are exhausted, to be recharged and sent forth again on its life-sustaining work.

Hence a Solar System is, to the Theosophist, not merely a splendid mechanism of physical matter, but the expression of a Life, and the nursery of lives derived therefrom, instinct in every part with latent or active intelligence, desire and activity. It "exists for the sake of the Self," in order that the germs of Divinity, the embryonic Selves emanated from the Supreme Self, may unfold into the likeness of the Parent-God, whose nature they share, being truly "partakers of the divine Nature." Its globes are "man-bearing," and not men alone but also sub-human beings, are its inhabitants. In worlds subtler than the physical dwell beings more highly evolved than men, as also beings less evolved; beings clothed in bodies of matter finer than the physical, and therefore invisible to physical eyes, but nonetheless active and intelligent; beings among whose hosts myriads of men are found, men who have, for the time, discarded their fleshly raiment, but who, none the less, are thinking, loving, active men. And even during life on our physical earth, encased in the garment of the flesh, men are in touch with these other worlds and other-world beings, and may be in conscious relation with them, as the Founders, Prophets, Mystics and Seers of all the faiths have witnessed.

The divine Lord manifests Himself in His System in three Aspects, or "Persons," the Creator, the Preserver, the Regenerator; these are the Holy Spirit, Son and Father of the Christian; the Brahma, Vishnu and Shiva of the Hindu; the Chokhmah,

Binah and Kether of the Hebrew Kabbalist; the Third, Second and First Logos of the Theosophist, who uses the old Greek term, "the WORD," for the manifested God.

The matter of the System is built up by the Third Logos, seven types of atoms being formed by Him; aggregations composed of these yield the seven fundamental kinds of matter found in the System, each denser than its predecessor, each kind being correlated with a distinct stage of Consciousness. We call the matter composed of a particular type of atom a plane or world, and hence recognise seven such planes in the Solar System: the two highest are the divine, or super-spiritual planes, the planes of Logoi, and the lower of these two is the birthplace and habitat of the human Self, the Monad, the God in Man; the two succeeding are the spiritual planes, reaching which man realises himself as divine; the fifth, still densifying, is the intellectual plane; the sixth, the emotional and passional, the seat of sensations and desires, is generally called the astral plane; the seventh, the physical plane. The matter of the spiritual planes is correlated with the spiritual stage of Consciousness, and is so subtle and so plastic that it yields to every impulse of the Spirit, and the sense of separateness is lost in that of unity. The matter of the intellectual plane is correlated with the intellectual stage of Consciousness, with Thought, Cognition, and every change in Thought is accompanied with a vibration of its matter. The late W.K. Clifford seems to have recognised "mind-stuff" as a

constituent of the cosmos, for, as every force needed
its medium, thought, regarded as a force, needed a
special kind of matter for its working. The matter of
the astral plane is correlated with the desire stage of
Consciousness, every change of emotion, passion,
desire, sensation being accompanied with a vibration of its matter. The matter of the physical plane is
the coarsest or densest, and is the first to be organ-
ized for the active expression of human Consciousness.

These seven kinds of matter, interpenetrating
each other—as physical solids, liquids, gases and
ethers interpenetrate each other in the objects round
us—are not all spread evenly over the whole area occupied by a Solar System, but are partly aggregated
into planets, worlds or globes; the three finest kinds
of matter do spread over the whole, and are thus
common to the system, but the four denser kinds
compose and surround the globes, and the fields
occupied by these are not in mutual touch.

We read in various Scriptures of "Seven Spirits":
Christianity and Islam have seven Archangels;
Zoroastrianism, seven Amshaspends; Judaism has
seven Sephiroth; Theosophy calls them the seven
planetary Logoi; and they are the Rulers of the
Planets Vulcan,* Venus, Earth, Jupiter, Saturn,
Uranus and Neptune.

Each of these seven Planets is the turning-point in
a chain of interlinked worlds, presided over by the

---

*Vulcan has not been discovered by scientists.

Planetary Logos, and each chain is a separate Field of Evolution from its earliest beginnings up to man. There are thus seven such subsidiary Fields of Evolution in a Solar System, and they are, naturally, at different stages of progress. The chain consists of seven globes, of which generally one is of physical and six of finer matter; in our own chain, however, our earth has two sister globes visible to physical sight—Mars and Mercury—and four invisible companions. The wave of evolutionary life, bearing the evolving beings, occupies one globe at a time—with certain special exceptions which need not be mentioned here—passing on to the next in order when the lessons on the earlier have been learned. Thus our humanity has travelled from globe 1, on the mental plane, to globe 2, on the astral; from that to globe 3, Mars, and to globe 4, our Earth; it will pass on to globe 5, Mercury, and from that to globe 6, again on the astral, and thence to globe 7, on the mental. This completes a great evolutionary Round, as it is aptly called.

This huge scheme of evolution cannot be readily grasped by the ignorant, any more than can the corresponding scheme of the astronomer, which deals only with the physical plane. Nor is it necessary that it should be understood by those of small intelligence, since it has no immediate bearing on life. It is interesting only to the man who, desiring to understand, is ready to grapple with the deeper problems of nature, and does not grudge strenuous intellectual exertion.

III

Man and His Worlds

*M*an is a spiritual Intelligence who has taken flesh with the object of gaining experience in worlds below the spiritual, in order that he may be able to master and to rule them, and in later ages take his place in the creative and directing Hierarchies of the universe.

There is a universal law that a Consciousness can only know that which it can reproduce; one Consciousness can know another in proportion as it is able to reproduce within itself the changes in that other. If a man feels pain when another man feels it, happiness when the other feels it, anxiety, confidence, etc., with the other, at once reproducing his moods, that man knows the other. Sympathy—feeling together—is the condition of knowledge. But

Consciousness works in bodies; we are clothed, not naked; and these bodies are composed of matter. Consciousness may affect Consciousness, but how can Consciousness affect these bodies?

There is another law, that a change in Consciousness is at once accompanied with a vibration in the matter near it, and each change has its own answering vibration, as a musical sound and a particular length and thickness of string invariably go together. In a Solar System all the separated Consciousnesses are part of the Consciousness of the divine Lord of the system, and all the matter of the system is His Body—"in Him we live and move and have our being." He has formed this matter and related to it Himself, so that it answers everywhere by innumerable kinds of vibrations to the innumerable changes in His Consciousness, each to each. Over His whole vast kingdom His Consciousness and His matter answer each other in perfect, perpetual harmony and inviolable relation.

Man shares with the divine Lord this relation, but in an elementary and feeble way; to the changes in his Consciousness answer vibrations in the matter around him, but this is only perfect and complete, at first, in the super-spiritual worlds, where he exists as an emanation from the Lord; there, every vibration of matter is answered by a change in his Consciousness, and he knows that world, his birthplace and his home. But in worlds of matter denser than that lofty region he is as yet a stranger; the vibrations of that denser matter, though all around him, do not affect him, are to him non-existent, as the waves which carry messages by wireless telegraphy do not affect us in this world, and are to our senses non-existent. How then can he grow to the likeness of his divine Parent, to whom every vibration has a message, who can set up any willed vibration in matter by a change in Consciousness, who is conscious and active at every point of His system?

The answer comes in the words: Involution and Evolution. He must involve himself in matter, attract to himself an encasement of matter, draw round himself materials from all the worlds—spiritual, intellectual, emotional and physical; this is the involving of Spirit in matter—Involution—sometimes called the descent of Spirit into matter, sometimes the fall of Man. Then, having acquired this encasement, he must slowly try to understand the changes in himself—in his own Consciousness—the surging, confusing, bewildering changes that come and go without any will of his, due to the vibrations set up in this material encasement of his by vibrations in the larger world around him, and that force upon his Consciousness unsought changes and moods. He has to disentangle these, to refer them to their proper origins, to learn through these the existence and the details of the surrounding worlds, to organise his own appropriated matter—his bodies—into more and more complex, receptive and discriminative agents, to admit to or shut out from these bodies at will the vibrations that hurtle round them outside, and at last, through them, to impress the changes in his Consciousness on external Nature, and thus to become its Ruler instead of its slave. This is Evolution, the ascent of the Spirit through matter, its unfolding within a material encasement drawn from the various worlds which form its environment. The spirit permeates with its own life the matter it appropriates, thus rendering it the docile servant of Spirit, and redeeming it from its cruder uses to the service of the liberated Sons of God.

This material encasement, drawn from the different worlds, must be gradually organised, by impacts from without and answers from within, into a "body," or a vehicle of Consciousness. It is organised from below, upwards, or from denser to finer, the materials from each world being organised separately, as a means of receiving communications from, and acting upon, its own world. The physical material is first drawn into a fairly compact mass, and the organs which carry on life processes, and those of the senses, are first slowly evolved; the wonderful and complicated physical body is evolved through millions of years, and is still evolving; it puts man into touch with the physical world around him, which he can see, hear, touch, taste and smell, and in which he can bring about changes by the use of his brain and nerves, directing and controlling his muscles, hands and feet. This body is not perfect, for there is still much in the physical world around it to which it cannot answer—forms, like atoms, which it cannot see, sounds which it cannot hear, and forces which it cannot perceive, till they have brought about effects by moving large masses of matter big enough for it to see. He has made delicate instruments to help his senses and to increase their perceptive range—telescopes and microscopes to help the eye, microphones to help the ear, galvanometers to find out forces which escape his senses. But presently the evolution of his own body will bring all his physical world within his ken.

Now that the physical body is highly organised, the next finer material, the astral, is being similarly evolved, and is bringing man gradually into touch with the astral—the emotional, passional, desire—world around him. Most modern people are becoming slightly conscious of astral impacts, while some are distinguishing them clearly. Premonitions, warnings, conscious touch with the ''dead,'' etc., all come from being open to impressions of the astral world.

The third state of matter, the mental, is also in course of organisation, and is putting man into touch with the intellectual world around him. As the mental body evolves the man comes into conscious relation with mental currents, with the minds of others near and distant, ''living'' and ''dead.''

The spiritual worlds still remain after this for man to conquer, and they have their appropriate body, the "spiritual body" of which S. Paul speaks. This organisation of matter to be the servant of Spirit is the part assigned to man in the great workshop of the worlds, and when the human stage is over there is nothing in the Solar System which he is incapable of knowing and affecting. He came forth from the divine Lord pure indeed, but ignorant and useless outside the subtle region of his birth; he returns, after his long pilgrimage, a wise and strong Son of God, ready to bear his part through the ages of the future as a minister of the divine Will in ever-widening fields of service.

IV

Man and His Mortal Bodies

*T*he Worlds in which man is evolving as he treads the circle of births and deaths are three: the physical world, the astral or intermediate world, the mental or heavenly world. In these three he lives from birth to death in his waking day-life; in the two latter he lives from birth to death in his sleeping night-life, and for a while after death; into the last he occasionally, but rarely, enters in his sleeping night-life, in high trance, and in it he spends the most important part of his life after death, the period spent there lengthening as he evolves.

The three bodies in which he functions in these worlds are all mortal; they are born and they die. They improve life after life, becoming more and more worthy to serve as the instruments of the unfolding Spirit. They are copies in denser matter of the undying spiritual bodies, which are unaffected by birth and death and form the clothing of the Spirit in the higher worlds, wherein he lives as the spiritual Man, while he lives here as the man of flesh, the ''carnal'' man. These undying spiritual bodies are that of which S. Paul speaks: ''We know that if our earthly house of this tabernacle were dissolved we have a building of God, an house not made with hands, eternal in the heavens. For in this we groan, earnestly desiring to be clothed upon with our house which is from heaven.'' These are the immortal bodies, and they will be dealt with in another chapter of this series.

The three mortal bodies are: the physical, the astral, and the mental, and they are related severally to the three worlds above-named.

The Physical Body

This is at present the most highly-developed body of man, and the one with which we are all familiar. It consists of solid, liquid, gaseous and etheric matter, the first three exquisitely organised into cells and tissues, these being built into organs which enable the consciousness to become aware of the outside world, and the latter possessing vortices through which forces pour. As the etheric part of the body separates at death from the solid, liquid and gaseous part, the physical body is often sub-divided into dense and etheric; the former is composed of the organs which receive and act; the latter is the medium of the life-forces and their transmitter to its dense comrade. Any tearing of the etheric part from the dense body during physical life is unwholesome; it is torn out by anaesthetics, and slips out, undriven, in some peculiar organisations, generally termed ''mediumistic''; apart from its denser comrade it is helpless and unconscious, a drifting cloud with force-centres, useless when there is nothing to which it can transmit the forces playing through it, and subject to manipulation from outside entities, who can use it as a matrix for materialisation. It cannot go far from the dense part of the body, since the latter would perish if disconnected from it; when disconnection occurs the dense part ''dies,'' *i.e.,* loses the inpouring of the vital forces which sustain its activities; even then the etheric part, or etheric double, hovers near its life-partner, and is the ''wraith,'' or ''shade,'' sometimes seen after death, drifting over graves. The physical body as a whole is man's medium for communication with the physical world, and it is sometimes called, for this reason, the ''body of action.'' It receives also vibrations from the subtler worlds, and when it is able to reproduce these it ''feels'' and ''thinks,'' its nervous system being organised to reproduce these in physical matter. As the viewless air, strongly vibrating, throws the denser water into ripples, as the viewless light throws the rods and cones of the retina into activity, so does the viewless matter of the subtler worlds throw into responsive vibrations the denser matter of our physical body, both etheric and dense. As evolution proceeds, and the physical body evolves, *i.e.,* appropriates finer and finer combinations of matter from the outside world, it becomes responsive to more and more rapid vibratory waves, and the man becomes more and more "sensitive." Racial evolution largely consists in this ever-increasing sensitiveness of the nervous system to outside impacts; for health, the sensitiveness must remain within limits of elasticity, *i.e.,* the system must immediately regain its normal condition after distortion; if this condition be present, such sensitiveness is on the crest of the evolutionary wave and makes possible the manifestation of genius; if it be not present, if equilibrium be not swiftly and spontaneously restored, then the sensitiveness is unhealthy and mischievous, leading to degeneration, and finally, if unchecked, to madness.

The Astral Body

The development of this body differs enormously in different persons, but in all it is the body which yields the experience of pleasure and pain, which is thrown into action by passion, desire and emotion, and in which reside the centres of our sense-organs—of sight, hearing, taste, smell and touch. If the passion, desire and emotion are low and sensual, then its matter is dense, its vibrations consequently are comparatively slow, and its colours are dark and unattractive—browns, dark reds and greens, and their combinations, lit from time to time with flashes of scarlet, which indicates a person at a lower stage of evolution. Brown-red indicates sensuality and greed; grey-green indicates deceit and cunning; brown indicates selfishness; scarlet indicates anger; yellow round head indicates intelligence; grey-blue above head indicates primitive religious feeling (fetish worship, etc.); touches of deep rose colour indicate beginning of love. As evolution goes on the matter becomes finer, and the colours clearer, purer and more brilliant. (See Plate I, Frontispiece, the developed astral body.) Green indicates sympathy and adaptability; rose indicates love; blue indicates religious feeling; yellow indicates intelligence; violet above the head indicates spirituality. These plates are not fanciful, but were drawn by an artist to the descriptions given by clairvoyant investigators.*

We are using this body throughout our waking hours, and in educated and refined people it has reached a fairly high state of evolution. Its finer matter is closely in touch with the matter of the mental body, and the two are constantly working together, acting and re-acting on each other. To gain a definite idea of these changes in the astral body, the reader should turn to Plates II and III which depict the influence of love and hate. Plate II illustrates

*These illustrations are reproduced from *Man, Visible and Invisible,* by C.W. Leadbeater, Quest Books, Theosophical Publishing House, Wheaton, IL, 1975.

some of the effects seen in the astral body of the man in love. The ordinary appearance of the astral body is transformed inasmuch as another human being has, for the time, become the centre of his world. Selfishness, deceit and anger have vanished, and an immense increase in the crimson colour of love is observable. Other undesirable changes there are, but it is an opening of the golden gates for the one who experiences it, and it is his fault if they close again. Plate III shows the terrible effects upon the astral body of intense anger; the whole organism is suffused by the black hue of malice and ill-will, which expresses itself in coils or vortices of thunderous blackness, from which fiery arrows of anger dart out, seeking to injure the one for whom the anger is felt—a tremendous and truly awful spectacle.

In sleep the astral body slips out of the physical, and in highly developed people the consciousness is functioning in the mental and higher bodies. We learn much during our sleep, and the knowledge thus gained slowly filters into the physical brain, and is occasionally impressed upon it as a vivid and illuminative dream. For the most part the consciousness in the astral world concerns itself little with the happenings there, being chiefly interested in its own exercise in thought and feeling; but it is possible to turn it outwards and to gain knowledge of the astral world. Communication with friends who have lost their physical bodies by death is constantly carried on there, and the memory may be brought back into waking consciousness, thus bridging the gulf otherwise made by death.

Premonitions, presentiments, the sensing of unseen presences and many allied experiences are due to the activity of the astral body and its reaction on the physical; their ever-increasing frequency is merely the result of its evolution among educated people. In a few generations it will be so generally developed that it will become as familiar as the physical body. After death we live for some time in the astral world in the astral body used during our life on earth, and the more we learn to control and use it wisely now, the better for us after death.

The Mental Body

This body, of finer material than the astral, as the astral is finer than the physical, is the body which answers by its vibrations to our changes of thought. Every change in thought makes a vibration in our mental body, and this, transmitted by the astral to the physical, causes activity in the nervous matter of our brains. This activity in the nervous cells causes many electrical and chemical changes in them, but it is the thought activity which causes these and not the changes which produce thought.

The mental body, like the astral, varies much in different people; it is composed of coarser or of finer matter according to the needs of the more or less unfolded consciousness connected with it. In the educated, it is active and well-defined; in the

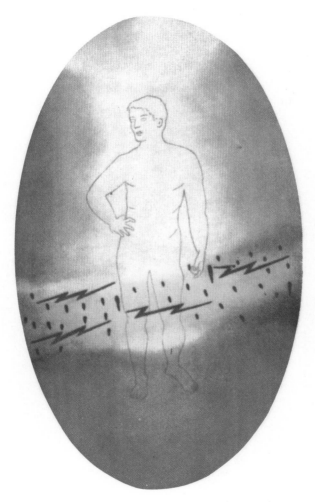

Plate II. The Astral Body of a Man in Love

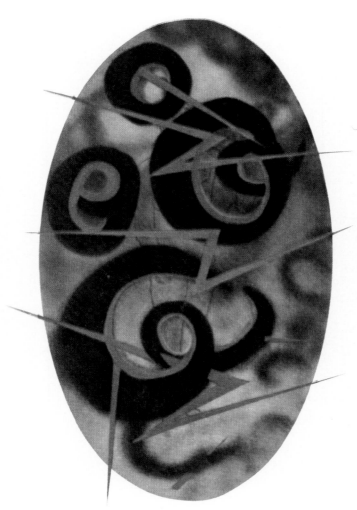

Plate III. The Astral Body in Intense Anger

undeveloped, it is cloudy and inchoate. Its matter, drawn from the mental plane, is that of the heaven-world, and it is continuously active, for man thinks in his waking consciousness when out of the physical body in sleep and after death, and lives wholly in thought and emotion when he leaves the astral world behind him and passes into heaven. As this is the body in which long centuries will be passed in the heaven-world, it is only rational to try to improve it as much as possible here. The means are study, thought, the exercise of good emotions, aspiration (prayer) and beneficent endeavours, and, above all, regular and strenuous meditation. The using of these will mean a rapid evolution of the mental body, and an immense enrichment of the heavenly life. Evil thoughts of all kinds befoul and injure it, and if persisted in, will become veritable diseases and maimings of the mental body, incurable during its period of life.

Such are man's three mortal bodies: he casts off the physical at death, the astral when ready to enter the heaven-world. When he has finished his heaven-life his mental body also disintegrates, and he is a Spirit clad in his immortal bodies. On descending for rebirth a new mental body is formed and a new astral, conformable to his character, and these attach themselves to his physical body, and he enters by birth on a new period of mortal life.

V

Man's Immortal Bodies

*W*e have a building of God, an house not made with hands, eternal in the heavens," said the great Christian Initiate S. Paul; "for in this [body] we groan, earnestly desiring to be clothed upon with our house which is from heaven." This heavenly house it is which is built of Man's immortal bodies, the habitation of the Spirit through unending ages, the dwelling place of man himself, through births and deaths, through the measureless period of his immortal life in manifestation.

The Spirit which is "the offspring of God" abides ever in the bosom of the Father, in very truth a Son of God, sharer in His eternal life. God made man "to be the image of His own eternity." This Spirit we call the Monad, because it is a unit, the very essence of Selfhood. The Monad, when he descends into matter in order to conquer and spiritualise it, appropriates to himself an atom of each of the three higher worlds, to make the nucleus of his three higher bodies—the super-spiritual, the spiritual and the intellectual. To these, by a thread of spiritual (buddhic) matter, he attaches also a particle from each of the three lower worlds, the nucleus of the three lower bodies.

For long, long ages he broods over these, as his future mortal bodies, just touched with his life, climb slowly upwards through the mineral, vegetable and animal kingdoms; meanwhile little aggregations of the matter of the three higher worlds, the "building of God . . . in the heavens" form a channel for his life, beginning to manifest in those worlds; and when the animal form has reached the point at which the upclimbing life makes strong appeal to the higher, he sends down through these an answering pulse of his life, and the intellectual body is suddenly completed, as light flashes out between the carbons of an electric arc. The man has individualised for life in the lower worlds.

The super-spiritual (atmic) body is but an atom of its lofty world, finest film of matter, embodiment of Spirit, "God made flesh" in a very real sense, divinity dipping down into the ocean of matter, not less divine because embodied. Gradually into this super-spiritual body will pass the pure result of all experiences, stored up in eternity, the two lower immortal bodies gradually merging themselves in it, blending with it, the glorious vesture of a man consciously divine, made perfect.

The spiritual (buddhic) body is of the second manifested world, the world of pure spiritual wisdom, knowledge and love in one, sometimes called the ''Christ-body,'' as it is this which is born into activity at the first great Initiation, and which develops to the ''fulness of the measure of the stature of Christ'' on the Path of Holiness. It is fed by all lofty and loving aspirations, by pure compassion and all-embracing tenderness and pity.

The intellectual (causal) body is the higher mind, by which the man deals with abstractions, which is ''of the nature of knowledge,'' in which he knows truth by intuition, not reasoning, borrowing from the lower mind ratiocinative methods only to establish in the lower world abstract truths which he himself knows directly. The man in this body is called the Ego, and when this body blends with the next above it, he is called the spiritual Ego, and begins to realize his own divinity. It is fed and developed by abstract thinking, by strenuous meditation, by dispassion, by the yoking of intellect to service. It is by nature separative, being the instrument of individualization, and must grow strong and self-sustaining in order to give the necessary stability to the subtle spiritual body with which it is to blend.

These are man's immortal bodies, subject neither to birth nor death; they give the continuous memory which is the essence of individuality; they are the treasure-house of all that deserves immortality; into them can enter "nothing that defileth"; they are the everlasting dwelling place of the Spirit. In these the promise is realized: "I will dwell in them and walk in them." These fulfil the prayer of the Christ: "That they also may be one in Us." These make good the triumphant cry of the Hindu: "I am Thou."

VI

The Law of Rebirth

Reincarnation in the Past

*T*here is, perhaps, no philosophical doctrine in the world that has so magnificent an intellectual ancestry as that of Reincarnation—the unfolding of the human Spirit through recurring lives on earth, experience being gathered during the earth life and worked up into intellectual faculty and conscience during the heaven-life, so that a child is born with his past experiences transmuted into mental and moral tendencies and powers. As Max Müller truly remarked, the greatest minds humanity has produced have accepted Reincarnation. Reincarnation is taught and illustrated in the great epics of the Hindus as an undoubted fact on which morality is based, and the splendid Hindu literature, which is

the admiration of European scholars, is permeated
with it. The Buddha taught it and constantly spoke
of his past births. Pythagoras did the same, and
Plato included it in his philosophical writings.
Josephus states that it was accepted among the Jews,
and relates the story of a captain who encouraged his
soldiers to fight to the death by reminding them of
their return to earth. In the *Wisdom of Solomon* it is
stated that coming into an undefiled body was the
reward of "being good." The Christ accepted it,
telling His disciples that John the Baptist was Elijah.
Virgil and Ovid take it for granted. The ritual composed by the learning of Egypt inculcated it. The
Neo-Platonic schools accepted it, and Origen, the
most learned of the Christian Fathers, declared that
"every man received a body according to his deserts
and his former actions." Though condemned by a
Roman Catholic Council, the heretical sects preserved the old tradition. And it comes to us in the
Middle Ages from a learned son of Islam: "I died
out of the stone and I became a plant; I died out of
the plant and I became an animal; I died out of the
animal and I became a man; why should I fear to
die? When did I grow less by dying? I shall die out
of the man and shall become an angel." In later
time we find it taught by Goethe, Fichte, Schelling,
Lessing, to name but some among the German
philosophers. Goethe in his old age looked joyfully
forward to his return; Hume declared that it was the
only doctrine of immortality a philosopher could

look at, a view somewhat similar to that of our British Professor McTaggart, who, reviewing the various theories of immortality, came to the conclusion that Reincarnation was the most rational. I need not remind any one of literary culture that Wordsworth, Browning, Rossetti and other poets believed it. The reappearance of the belief in Reincarnation is not, therefore, an emergence of a superstitious belief among civilized nations, but a sign of recovery from a temporary mental aberration in Christendom, from the derationalization of religion which has wrought so much evil and has given rise to so much skepticism and materialism. To assert the special creation of a soul for every fresh body, implying that the coming into existence of a soul depends on the formation of a body, inevitably leads to the conclusion that with the death of the body the soul will pass out of existence; that a soul with no past should have an everlasting future is as incredible as that a stick should exist with only one end. Only a soul which is unborn can hope to be undying. The loss of the teaching of Reincarnation—with its temporary purgatory for working out evil passions and its temporary heaven for the transmutation of experience into faculty—gave rise to the idea of a never-ending heaven for which no one is good enough, and a never-ending hell for which no one is wicked enough, confined human evolution to an inappreciable fragment of existence, hung an everlasting future on the contents of a few years, and made life an unintelligible tangle of injustices and partialities, of unearned genius and unmerited criminality, an intolerable problem to the thoughtful, tolerable only to blind and foundationless faith.

Reincarnation and Its Necessity

There are but three explanations of human inequalities, whether of faculties, of opportunities, of circumstances: I. Special creation by God, implying that man is helpless, his destiny being controlled by an arbitrary and incalculable will. II. Heredity, as suggested by science, implying an equal helplessness on man's part, he being the result of a past over which he had no control. III. Reincarnation, implying that man can become master of his destiny, he being the result of his own individual past, being what he has made himself.

Special creation is rejected by all thoughtful people as an explanation of the conditions round us, save in the most important conditions of all, the character with which and the environment into which an infant is born. Evolution is taken for granted in everything except in the life of spiritual intelligence called man; he has no individual past, although he has an individual endless future. The character he brings with him—on which more than on anything else his destiny on earth depends—is, on this hypothesis, specially created for him by God, and imposed on him without any choice of his own, out of the lucky bag of creation he may draw a prize or a blank, the blank being a doom of misery; such as it is, he must take it.

If he draw a good disposition, fine capacities, a noble nature, so much the better for him; he has done nothing to deserve them. If he draw congenital criminality, congenital idiocy, congenital disease, congenital drunkenness, so much the worse for him; he has done nothing to deserve them. If everlasting bliss be tacked on to the one and everlasting torment to the other, the unfortunate one must accept his ill fate as he may. Hath not the potter power over the clay? Only it seems sad if the clay be sentient.

In another respect special creation is grotesque. A spirit is specially created for a small body which dies a few hours after birth. If life on earth has any educational or experimental value, that spirit will be the poorer forever by missing such a life, and the lost opportunity can never be made good. If, on the other hand, human life on earth is of no essential importance and carries with it the certainty of many ill-doings and sufferings and the possibility of everlasting suffering at the end of it, the spirit that comes into a body that endures to old age is hardly dealt with, as it must endure innumerable ills escaped by the other without any equivalent advantage, and may be damned forever.

The list of injustices brought about by the idea of special creation might be extended indefinitely, for it includes all inequalities. It has made myriads of atheists, who consider it incredible to the intelligence and revolting to the conscience. It places man in the position of the inexorable creditor of God, stridently demanding: "Why has thou made me thus?"

The glory of humanity, from the scientific standpoint, seems outside the law of causation. Science does not tell us how to build strong minds and pure hearts for the future. She does not threaten us with an arbitrary will, but she leaves us without explanation of human inequalities. She tells us that the drunkard bequeaths to his children bodies prone to disease, but she does not explain why some unhappy children are the recipients of the hideous legacy.

Reincarnation restores justice to God and power to man. Every human spirit enters into human life a germ, without knowledge, without conscience, without discrimination. By experience, pleasant and painful, man gathers materials, and as before explained, builds them into mental and moral faculties. Thus the character he is born with is self-made, and marks the stage he has reached in his long evolution. The good disposition, the fine capacities, the noble nature are the spoils of many a hard fought field, the wages of heavy and arduous toil. The reverse marks an early stage of growth, the small development of the spiritual germ.

All tread a similar road; all are destined to ultimate human perfection. Pain follows on mistakes and is ever remedial; strength is developed by struggle; we reap after every sowing the inevitable result—happiness growing out of the right, sorrow out of the wrong. The babe dying shortly after birth pays in the death a debt owing from the past and returns swiftly to earth, delayed but for brief space and free of his debt to gather the experience necessary for his growth. Social virtues, though placing a man at a disadvantage in the struggle for existence, perhaps even leading to the sacrifice of his physical life, build a noble character for his future lives and shape him to become a servant of the nation.

Genius inheres in the individual as the result of many lives of effort, and the sterility of the body it wears does not rob the future of its services, as it returns greater on every rebirth. The body poisoned by a father's drunkenness is taken by a spirit learning by a lesson of suffering to guide its earthly life on lines better than those followed in the past.

And so in every case the individual past explains the individual present, and when the laws of growth are known and obeyed a man can build with a sure hand his future destiny, shaping his growth on lines of ever-increasing beauty until he reaches the stature of the Perfect Man.

Why our Past Lives Are Forgotten

No question is more often heard when reincarnation is spoken of than: "If I were here before, why do I not remember it?" A little consideration of facts will answer the question.

First of all, let us note the fact that we forget more of our present lives than we remember. Many people cannot remember learning to read: yet the fact that they can read proves the learning. Incidents of childhood and youth have faded from our memory, yet they have left traces on our character. A fall in babyhood is forgotten, yet the victim is nonetheless a cripple, although using the same body in which the forgotten events were experienced.

These events, however, are not wholly lost by us; if a person be thrown into a mesmeric trance, they may be drawn from the depths of memory; they are submerged, not destroyed. Fever patients have been known to use in delirium a language known in childhood and forgotten in maturity. Much of our sub-consciousness consists of these submerged experiences, memories thrown into the background but recoverable.

If this be true of experiences encountered in the present body, how much more must it be true of experiences encountered in former bodies, which died and decayed many centuries ago? Our present body and brain have had no share in those far-off happenings; how should memory assert itself through them? Our permanent body, which remains with us throughout the cycle of reincarnation, is the spiritual body; the lower garments fall away and return to their elements ere we can become reincarnated.

The new mental, astral and physical matter in which we are reclothed for a new life on earth receives from the spiritual intelligence, garbed only in the spiritual body, not the experiences of the past but the qualities, tendencies and capacities which have been made out of those experiences. Our conscience, our instinctive response to emotional and intellectual appeals, or recognition of the force of a logical argument, our assent to fundamental principles of right and wrong, these are the traces of past experience. A man of a low intellectual type cannot "see" a logical or mathematical proof; a man of low moral type cannot "feel" the compelling force of a high moral ideal.

When a philosophy or a science is quickly grasped and applied, when an art is mastered without study, memory is there in power, though past facts of learning are forgotten; as Plato said, it is reminiscence. When we feel intimate with a stranger on first meeting, memory is there, the spirit's recognition of a friend of ages past; when we shrink back with strong repulsion from another stranger, memory is there, the spirit's recognition of an ancient foe.

These affinities, these warnings, come from the undying spiritual intelligence which is our self; we remember, though working in the brain we cannot impress on it our memory. The mind-body, the brain, are new; the spirit furnishes the mind with the results of the past, not with the memory of its events. As a merchant, closing the year's ledger and opening a new one, does not enter in the new one all the items of the old but only its balances, so does the spirit hand on to the new brain his judgments on the experiences of a life that is closed, the conclusions to which he has come, the decisions at which he has arrived. This is the stock handed on to the new life, the mental furniture for the new dwelling—a real memory.

Rich and varied are these in the highly evolved man; if these are compared with the possessions of the younger soul, the value of such a memory of a long past is patent. No brain could store the memory of the events of numerous lives; when they are concreted into mental and moral judgments they are available for use. Hundreds of murders have led up to the decision "I must not kill"; the memory of each murder would be a useless burden, but the judgment based on their results, the instinct of the sanctity of human life, is the effective memory of them in the civilized man.

Memory of past events, however, is sometimes found; children have occasional fleeting glimpses of their past, recalled by some event of the present. An English boy who had been a sculptor recalled it when he first saw some statues. An Indian child recognised a stream in which he had been drowned as a little child in a preceding life, and the mother of that earlier body. Many cases are on record of such memory of past events.

Moreover, such memory can be gained. But the gaining is a matter of steady effort, of prolonged meditation, whereby the restless mind, ever running outwards, may be controlled and rendered quiescent, so that it may be sensitive and responsive to the Spirit and receive from him the memory of the past. Only as we can hear the still small voice of the Spirit may the story of the past be unrolled, for the Spirit alone can remember, and cast down the rays of his memory to enlighten the darkness of the fleeting lower nature to which he is temporarily attached.

Under such conditions memory is possible, links of the past are seen, old friends recognised, old scenes recalled, and a subtle strength and calm grows out of the practical experience of immortality. Present troubles grow light when seen in their true proportions as trivial and transient events in an unending life; present joys lose their brilliant colours when seen as repetitions of past delights; and both alike are equally accepted as useful experiences, enriching mind and heart and contributing to the growth of the unfolding life.

Not until pleasure and pain, however, have been seen in the light of eternity can the crowding memories of the past be safely confronted; when they have thus been seen, then those memories calm the emotions of the present, and that which would otherwise have crushed becomes a support and consolation. Goethe rejoiced that on his return to earth-life he would be washed clean of his memories, and lesser men may be content with the wisdom which starts each new life on its way, enriched with the results, but unburdened with the recollections of its past.

VII

The Riddle of Love and Hate

*T*o the great majority of us life presents a series of tangles and puzzles—tangles we cannot unravel, puzzles we cannot solve. Why are people born differing so widely in mental and in moral capacity? Why has one infant a brain denoting great intellectual and moral power, while another has a brain which marks him out as one who will be an idiot or a criminal? Why has one child good and loving parents and favourable circumstances, while another has profligate parents who detest him, and is reared amid the foulest surroundings? Why is one "lucky" and another "unlucky"? Why does one die old and another die young? Why is one person prevented by "accidents" from catching a steamer or a train that is wrecked, while scores or hundreds of others perish unaided? Why do we like one person the moment we see him, while we as promptly dislike another? Questions like these are continually arising, and are as continually left unanswered, and yet answers are within reach; for all these seeming incongruities and injustices, these apparently fortuitous events, are merely the results of the working out of a few simple and fundamental natural laws. An understanding of these underlying laws makes life intelligible, thereby restoring our confidence in the divine order and endowing us with strength and courage to meet the vicissitudes of fortune. Troubles which strike us like "bolts from the blue" are hard to bear, but troubles which arise from causes we can understand, and can therefore control, can be faced with patience and resignation.

The first principle that must be firmly grasped ere we can begin to apply it to the solving of life's problems is that of Reincarnation. Man is essentially a Spirit, a living and self-conscious individual, consisting of this self-conscious life in a body of very subtle matter; life cannot work without a body of some kind; that is, without a form of matter, however fine and subtle the matter may be, which gives it separate existence in this universe; the body is often therefore spoken of as a vehicle, that which carries the life, making it individual. This Spirit, when he comes into the physical world by the gateway of birth, puts on a physical body as a man puts on an overcoat and hat to go out into the world beyond his own home; but the physical body is no

more the man than the overcoat and hat are the
body which wears them. As a man throws away
worn-out garments and puts on new ones, so does
the Spirit cast off a worn-out body and take to
himself another (*Bhagavad-Gita*). When the physical
body is outworn the man passes through the gateway
of death, dropping the physical vesture and entering
the "unseen" world. After a long period of rest and
refreshment, during which the experiences of the
past life on earth are assimilated and thus increase
the powers of the man, he returns again to the
physical world through the gateway of birth and
takes on a new physical body, adapted for the
expression of his increased capacities. When Spirits
which were to become human came into the world
millennia ago, they were but embryos, like seeds,
knowing neither good nor evil, with infinite
possibilities of development—as being the offspring
of God—but without any actual powers save that of
thrilling feebly in response to external stimuli. All
the powers latent within them had to be roused into
active manifestation by experiences undergone in
the physical world. By pleasure and pain, by joy and
suffering, by success and failure, by fruition and
disappointment, by successive choices well and
badly made, the Spirit learns his lessons of laws that
cannot be broken, and manifests slowly one by one
his capacities for mental and moral life. After each
brief plunge into the ocean of physical life—that
period generally spoken of as "a life"—he returns to

the invisible world laden with the experiences he has gathered, as a diver rises from the sea with the pearls he has riven from the oyster-bed. In that invisible world he transmutes into moral and mental powers all the moral and mental materials he has gathered in the earth-life just closed, changing aspirations into capacity to achieve, changing the results of efforts that failed into forces for future success, changing the lessons of mistakes into prudence and foresight, changing past sufferings into endurance, changing errors into repulsions from wrong-doings, and the sum of experience into wisdom. As Edward Carpenter well wrote: ''All the pains that I suffered in one body became powers that I wielded in the next.''

When all that was gathered has been assimilated—the length of the heavenly life depending on the amount of mental and moral material that had been collected—the man returns to earth; he is guided, under conditions to be explained in a moment, to the race, the nation, the family, which is to provide him with his next physical body, and the body is moulded in accordance with his requirements, so as to serve as a fit instrument for his powers, as a limitation which expresses his deficiencies. In the new physical body, and in the life in the invisible world that follows its off-throwing at the death which destroys it, he re-treads on a higher level a similar cycle, and so again and again for hundreds of lives, until all his possibilities as a human being have become active powers, and he has learned every lesson that this human life can teach. Thus the Spirit unfolds from infancy to youth, from youth to maturity, becoming an individualized life of immortal strength and of boundless utility for divine service. The struggling and unfolding Spirits of one humanity become the guardians of the next humanity, the spiritual Intelligences that guide the evolution of worlds posterior to their own in time. We are protected, helped and taught by spiritual Intelligences who were men in worlds older than our own, as well as by the most highly evolved men of our own humanity; we shall repay the debt by protecting, helping and teaching human races in worlds that are now in the early stages of their growth, preparing to become, untold ages hence, the homes of future men. If we find around us many who are ignorant, stupid and even brutal, limited in both mental and moral powers, it is because they are younger men than we are, younger brothers, and hence their errors should be met with love and helpfulness instead of with bitterness and hatred. As they are, so were we in the past; as we are, so shall they be in the future; and both they and we shall go onward and onward through the everlasting ages.

This then is the first fundamental principle which renders life intelligible when applied to the conditions of the present; I can only work out from it in detail here the answer to one of the questions propounded above, namely, why we like one person and dislike another at sight; but all the other questions might be answered in similar fashion. For the complete answering, however, we need to grasp also the twin principle of Reincarnation—that of Karma, or the Law of Causation.

This may be stated in words familiar to all: "Whatsoever a man soweth, that shall he also reap." Amplifying this brief axiom, we understand by it that a man forms his own character, becoming that which he thinks; that he makes the circumstances of his future life by the effects of his actions upon others. Thus, if I think nobly I shall gradually make for myself a noble character, but if I think basely, a base character will be formed. "Man is created by thought; that which he thinks upon in one life he becomes in another," as a Hindu scripture has it. If the mind dwells continually on one train of thought, a groove is formed into which the thought-force runs automatically, and such a habit of thought survives death, and, since it belongs to the Ego, is carried over to the subsequent earth-life as a thought-tendency and capacity. Habitual study of abstract problems, to take a very high instance, will result, in another earth-life, in a well-developed power for abstract thinking, while flippant, hasty thinking, flying from one subject to another, will bequeath a restless, ill-regulated mind to the following birth into this world. Selfish coveting of the possessions of others, though never carried out into active cheating in the present, makes the thief of a later earth-life, while hatred and revenge, secretly cherished, are the seeds from which the murderers spring. So again, unselfish loving yields as harvest the philanthropist and the saint, and every thought of compassion helps to build the tender and pitiful nature which belongs to one who is "a friend to all creatures." The knowledge of this law of changeless justice, of the exact response of nature to every demand, enables a man to build his character with all the certainty of science, and to look forward with courageous patience to the noble type he is gradually but surely evolving.

The effects of our actions upon others mould the external circumstances of a subsequent earth-life. If we have caused widespread happiness, we are born into very favourable physical surroundings or come into them during life, while the causing of widespread misery results in an unhappy environment. We make relationships with others by coming into contact with them individually, and bonds are forged by benefits and injuries, golden links of love or iron chains of hate. This is Karma. With these complementary ideas clearly in mind, we can answer our question very easily.

Links between Egos, between individualized Spirits, cannot antedate the first separation of those Spirits from the Logos, as drops may be separated from the ocean. In the mineral and vegetable kingdoms, the life that expresses itself in stones and plants has not yet evolved into continued individualized existence. The word "group soul" has been used to express the idea of this evolving life as it animates a number of similar physical organisms. Thus a whole order, say of plants, like grasses, umbelliferous or rosaceous plants, is animated by a single group-soul, which evolves by virtue of the simple experiences gathered through its countless physical embodiments. The experiences of each plant flow into the life that informs its whole order and aid and hasten its evolution. As the physical embodiments become more complex, sub-divisions are set up in the group-soul, and each sub-division slowly and gradually separates off, the number of embodiments belonging to each subdivisional group-soul thus formed diminishing as these subdivisions increase. In the animal kingdom this process of specialization of the group-souls continues, and in the higher mammalia a comparatively small number of creatures is animated by a single group-soul, for Nature is working toward individualization. The experiences gathered by each are preserved in the group-soul, and from it affect each newly-born animal that it informs; these appear as what we call instincts, and are found in the newly-born creature. Such is the instinct which makes a newly-hatched chicken fly to seek protection from danger under the brooding wing of the hen, or that which impels the beaver to build its dam. The accumulated experiences of its species, preserved in the group-soul, inform every member of the group.

When the animal kingdom reaches its highest expressions, the final subdivisions of the group-soul animate but a single creature, until finally the divine life pours out anew into this vehicle now ready for its reception, and the human Ego takes birth and the evolution of the self-conscious intelligence begins.

From the time that a separated life animates a single body, links may be set up with other separated lives, each likewise dwelling in a single tabernacle of flesh. Egos, dwelling in physical bodies, come into touch with each other; perhaps a mere physical attraction draws together two Egos dwelling respectively in male and female bodies. They live together, have common interests, and thus links are set up. If the phrase may be allowed, they contract debts to each other, and there are no bankruptcy courts in Nature where such liabilities may be cancelled. Death strikes away one body, then the other, and the two have passed into the invisible world; but debts contracted on the physical plane must be discharged in the world to which they belong, and those two must meet each other again in earth-life and renew the intercourse that was broken off. The great spiritual Intelligences who administer the law of Karma guide these two into rebirth at the same period of time, so that their earthly lifetimes may overlap, and in due course they meet. If the debt contracted be a debt of love and of mutual service, they will feel attracted to each other; the Egos recognise each other, as two friends recognise each other, though each be wearing a new dress, and they clasp hands, not as strangers but as friends. If the debt be one of hatred and of injury, they shrink apart with a feeling of repulsion, each recognising an ancient enemy, eyeing each other across the gulf of wrongs given and received. Cases of these types must be known to every reader, although the underlying cause has not been known; and indeed these sudden likings and dislikings have often foolishly been spoken of as "causeless," as though, in a world of law, anything could be without a cause. It by no means follows that Egos thus linked together necessarily re-knit the exact relationship broken off down here by the hand of death. The husband and wife of one earth-life might be born into the same family as brother and sister, as father and son, as father and daughter, or in any other blood relationship. Or they might be born as strangers, and meet for the first time in youth or in maturity, to feel for each other an over-mastering attraction. In how brief a time we become closely intimate with one who was a stranger, while we live beside another for years and remain aliens in heart! Whence these strange affinities, if they are not the remembrances in the Egos of the loves of their past? "I feel as if I had known you all my life," we say to a friend of a few weeks, while others whom we have known all our lives are to us as sealed books. The Egos know each other, though the bodies be strangers, and the old friends clasp hands in perfect confidence and understand each other; and this, although the physical brains have not yet learned to receive those impressions of memory that exist in the subtle bodies, but that are too fine to cause vibrations in the gross matter of the brain, and thus to awaken responsive thrills of consciousness in the physical body.

Sometimes the links, being of hatred and wrong-doing, draw together ancient enemies into one family, there to work out in misery the evil results of the common past. Ghastly family tragedies have their roots deep down in the past, and many of the awful facts, the torture of helpless children even by their own mothers, the malignant ferocity which inflicts pain in order to exult in the sight of agony—all this becomes intelligible when we know that the soul in that young body has in the past inflicted some horror on the one who now torments it, and is learning by terrible experience how hard are the ways of wrong.

The question may arise in the minds of some: "If this be true, ought we to rescue the children?" Most surely, yes. It is our duty to relieve suffering wherever we meet it, rejoicing that the Good Law uses us as its almoners of mercy.

Another question may come: How can these links of evil be broken? Will not the torture inflicted forge a new bond, by which the cruel parent will hereafter be the victim, and the tortured child become the oppressor? "Hatred ceases not by hatred at any time," quotes the Lord Buddha, knowing the law. But He breathed the secret of release when He continued: "Hatred ceases by love." When the Ego who has paid his debt of the past by the suffering of inflicted wrong is wise enough, brave enough, great enough to say, amid the agony of body and mind: "I forgive!" then he cancels the debt he might have wrung from his ancient foe, and the bond forged by hate melts away forever in the fire of love.

The links of love grow strong in every successive earth-life in which the linked two clasp hands, and they have the added advantage of growing stronger during the life in heaven, whereinto the links of hate cannot be carried. Egos that have debts of hate between them do not touch each other in the heavenly land, but each works out such good as he may have in him without contact with his foe.

When the Ego succeeds in impressing on the brain of his physical body his own memory of his past, then these memories draw the Egos yet closer, and the tie gains a sense of security and strength such as no bond of a single life can give; very deep and strong is the happy confidence of such Egos, knowing by their own experiences that love does not die.

Such is the explanation of affinities and repulsions, seen in the light of Reincarnation and Karma.

VIII

Karma—The Law of Action and Reaction

*T*he word "Karma" simply means Action. But the connotation of the word is far-reaching, for much more goes to the making of an action than the ordinary person might think. Every action has a past which leads up to it; every action has a future which proceeds from it; an action implies a desire which prompted it and a thought which shaped it, as well as a visible movement to which the name of "act" is usually confined. Each act is a link in an endless chain of causes and effects, each effect becoming a cause, and each cause having been an effect; and each link in this endless chain is welded out of three components, desire, thought and activity. A desire stimulates a thought; a thought embodies itself in an act. Sometimes it is a thought, in the form of a memory, that arouses a desire, and the desire bursts into an act. But ever the three components—two invisible and belonging to consciousness, one visible and belonging to the body—are there; to speak with perfect accuracy, the act is also in consciousness as an image before it is extruded as a physical movement. Desire—or Will—Thought, Activity, are the three modes of consciousness.

This relation of desire, thought and activity as "Action," and the endless interlinkings of such actions as causes and effects, are all included under the word Karma. It is a recognised succession in nature, *i.e.*, a Law. Hence Karma may be Anglicised into "Causation," or the Law of Causation. Its scientific statement is: "Action and Reaction are equal and opposite." Its religious statement cannot be better put than in the well-known verse of a Christian Scripture: "As as man soweth, so shall he also reap." Sometimes it is called the Law of Equilibrium, because whenever equilibrium is disturbed, there is a tendency in nature to restore the condition of equilibrium.

Karma is thus the expression of the Divine Nature in its aspect to Law. It is written: "In whom there is no variableness, neither shadow of turning." The inviolableness of natural order; the exactitude of natural law; the utter trustworthiness of nature—these are the strong foundations of the universe. Without these there could be no science, no certitude, no reasoning from the past, no presaging of the future. Human experience would become useless, and life would be a chaotic irrationality.

What a man sows, he reaps. That is Karma. If he wants rice, he must sow rice. Useless to plant vines and to expect roses; idle to sow thistledown and hope for wheat. In the moral and the mental worlds, law is equally changeless; useless to sow idleness, and hope to reap learning; to sow carelessness, and look for discretion; to sow selfishness, and expect love; to sow fear and hope for courage. This sane and true teaching bids man study the causes he is setting up by his daily desires, thoughts and actions, and realize their inevitable fruiting. It bids him surrender all the fallacious ideas of "forgiveness," "vicarious atonement," "divine mercy," and the rest of the opiates which superstition offers to the sinner. It cries out as with a trumpet blast to all those who thus seek to drug themselves into peace: "Be not deceived; God is not mocked; *whatsoever* a man soweth *that* shall he also reap."

That is the warning side of the law but note the encouraging. If there is a law in the mental and moral world we can build our character; thought makes quality; quality makes character. "As a man thinks so he is." "Man is created by thought; what a man thinks upon, that he becomes." If we meditate on courage, we shall work courage into our character. So with purity, patience, unselfishness, self-control. Steady, persevering thought sets up a definite habit of the mind, and that habit manifests itself as a quality in the character. We can build our character as surely as a mason can build a wall, working with and through the law. Character is the most powerful factor in destiny, and by building a noble character, we can ensure a destiny of usefulness, of service to mankind. As by law we suffer, so by law do we triumph. Ignorance of law leaves us as the rudderless boat drifting on the current. Knowledge of law gives us a helm by which we can steer our ship wherever we will.

IX

The Three Threads of the Cord of Fate

*T*o the Greek there were three Fates who spun the cord of life. To the knower of the Wisdom there are three Fates also, each of them ever spinning a thread, and the three threads they spin are twisted into one, and form the strong cord of Destiny which binds or loosens man's life on earth. These three Fates are not the women of the Greek legend; they are the three Powers of the human Consciousness; the Power to Will, the Power to Think, the Power to Act. These are the Fates which spin the threads of human destiny, and they are within the man, not outside him. Man's destiny is self-made, not imposed upon him arbitrarily from without; his own powers, blinded by ignorance, spin and twist the cord that fetters him, as his own powers, directed by knowledge, liberate his limbs from the self-imposed shackles and set him free from bondage.

The most important of these three Powers is his Power to Think; *man* means thinker; it is a Sanskrit root, and from this are derived the English *man*—identical with the Sanskrit root—the German *Mann,* the French *homme,* the Italian *uomo,* etc. The thread of thought is woven into mental and moral qualities, and these qualities in their totality form what we call character. This connection of thought and character is recognised in the scriptures of nations. In the Bible we read: "As a man thinks, so is he." This is the general law. More particularly: "He that looketh upon a woman to lust after her, *hath committed adultery* already with her in his heart." Or: "He that hateth his brother *is* a murderer." On the same lines declares an Indian scripture: "Man is created by thought; as a man thinks, so he becomes." Or: "A man consists of his belief; as he believes, so is he." The *rationale* of these facts is that when the mind is turned to a particular thought and dwells on it, a definite vibration of matter is set up, and the oftener this vibration is caused the more does it tend to repeat itself, to become a habit, to become automatic. The body follows the mind and imitates its changes; if we concentrate our thought, the eyes become fixed, the muscles tense; an effort to remember is accompanied with a frown; the eyes rove hither and thither, as we seek to recover a lost impression; anxiety, anger, love, impatience, have all their appropriate muscular accompaniments; the feeling which makes a man inclined to throw himself from a height is the inclination of the body to act out the thought of falling. The first step towards a deliberate creation of character lies, then, in the deliberate choosing of what we will think, and then of thinking persistently on the quality chosen. Ere long there will be a tendency to show that quality; a little longer, and its exercise will have become habitual. We spin the thread of Thought into our destiny, and find ourselves with a character bent to all noble and useful ends. As we have thought, we have become. *Thought makes character.*

The Power to will is the second Fate, and spins a strong thread for the cord of destiny. Will shows itself as desire: desire to possess, which is love, attraction, in innumerable forms; desire to repel, which is hate, repulsion, driving away that which is to us undesirable. As truly as the magnet attracts and holds soft iron, so does our desire to attract draw to us that which we wish to possess and hold as ours. The strong desire for wealth and success brings them into our grasp; what we will to have, steadily and persistently, that comes to us sooner or later. Fleeting, indeterminate, changing fancies, these have but little attractive force; but the man of strong will obtains that which he wills. This thread of will brings us objects of desire and opportunities for gaining them. *Will makes opportunities and attracts objects.*

The third thread is spun by the Power to Act, and this is the thread which brings into our destiny outward happiness or outward misery. As we act towards those around us, so do they re-act upon us. The man who spreads happiness round him feels happiness flowing in upon himself; he who makes others unhappy feels the re-action of unhappiness upon himself. Smiles beget smiles; frowns, frowns; an irritable person arouses irritability in others. The law of the spinning of this thread is: *Our actions affecting others cause a reaction of a similar nature on ourselves.*

These are the threads which make destiny, for they make character, opportunity and environment; they are not cut short by death, but stretch onwards into other lives; the thread of thought gives us the character with which we are born into the world; the thread of will brings or withholds opportunities, makes us ''lucky'' or ''unlucky''; the thread of act brings us favourable or unfavourable physical conditions. As we are sowing, so shall we reap; as we are spinning, so shall be destiny's cord in the future. Man is the Creator of his Future; man is the Maker of his Destiny; man is his own Fate.

X

Thought-Power and Its Use

*O*ne of the most striking features of the present day is the recognition on all hands of the power of thought, the belief that a man can mould his character, and therefore his destiny, by the exercise of this power which makes him man. In this our modern ideas are coming into line with the religious teachings of the past. "Man is created by thought," was written in a Hindu scripture. "What a man thinks on that he becomes; therefore think on the Eternal." "As he thinketh in his heart, so he is," said the wise King of Israel, giving warning against association with an evil man. "All that we are is made up of our thoughts," said the Buddha. Thought is the parent of action; our nature sets itself to embody that which is generated by thought.

Modern psychology states that the body tends to follow out the thought, and traces the inclination felt by some to throw themselves down from a height to the imagination picturing a fall, and the body acting out the picture.

There being, then, an appreciation of the Power of Thought, it becomes a matter of great moment to know how to use this power in the highest possible way and to the greatest possible effect. This can best be done by the practice of meditation, and one of the simplest methods—which has also the advantage that its value can be tested by each person for himself—is as follows.

Examining your own character, you pick some distinct defect in it. You then ask yourself, what is its exact opposite, the virtue which is its antithesis. Let us say that you suffer from irritability; you select patience. Then, regularly every morning, before going out into the world, you sit down for from three to five minutes and think on patience—its value, its beauty, its practice under provocation, taking one point one day, another, another, and thinking as steadily as you can, recalling the mind when it wanders; think of yourself as perfectly patient, a model of patience, and end with a vow, "This Patience, which is my true Self, I will feel and show today."

For a few days, probably, there will be no change perceptible; you will still feel and show irritability. Go on steadily every morning. Presently, as you say an irritable thing, the thought will flash into your mind unbidden, "I should have been patient." Still go on. Soon the thought of patience will arise *with* the irritable impulse, and the outer manifestation will be checked. Still go on. The irritable impulse will grow feebler and feebler, until you find that irritability has disappeared, and that patience has become your normal attitude towards annoyances.

Here is an experiment that anyone can try, and prove the law for himself. Once proven, he can use it, and build virtue after virtue in a similar way, until he has created an ideal character by the Power of Thought.

Another use for this power is to help any good cause by sending to it good thoughts; to aid a friend in trouble by sending thoughts of comfort; a friend in search of truth by thoughts, clear and definite, of the truths you know. You can send out into the mental atmosphere thoughts which will raise, purify, inspire, all who are sensitive to them; thoughts of protection, to be guardian angels of those you love. Right thought is a continual benediction which each can radiate, like a fountain spraying forth sweet waters.

Yet must we not forget the reverse of this fair picture. Wrong thought is as swift for evil as is right thought for good. Thought can wound as well as heal, distress as well as comfort. Ill thoughts thrown into the mental atmosphere poison receptive minds; thoughts of anger and revenge lend strength to the murderous blow; thoughts which wrong others barb the tongue of slander, wing the arrows loosed at the unjustly assailed. The mind tenanted by evil thoughts acts as a magnet to attract like thoughts from others, and thus intensifies the original ill. To think on evil is a step towards doing evil, and a polluted imagination prompts the realization of its own foul creations. "As a man thinks so he becomes," is the law for evil thoughts as well as for good. Moreover, to dwell on an evil thought gradually deprives it of its repulsiveness, and impels the thinker to perform an action which embodies it.

Such is the Law of Thought, such its power. "If ye know these things, happy are ye if ye do them."

XI

Steps on the Path

The normal course of human evolution leads man upwards, stage by stage. But an immense distance separates even the genius and the saint from the man who "stands on the threshold of divinity"—still more from him who has fulfilled the Christ's command: "Be ye perfect, as your Father in heaven is perfect." Are there any steps which lead up to the gateway of which it is written: "Strait is the gate and narrow is the way that leadeth unto life, and few there be that find it?" Who are "the perfect," of whom Paul the Apostle speaks?

Truly are there steps which lead up to that Portal, and there are few which tread that narrow way. The Gate is the Gate of Initiation, the second birth, the baptism of the Holy Ghost and of Fire; the Way leads to the knowledge of God which is life in the Eternal.

In the Western world, the stages or steps, have been called: Purgation, Illumination, Union; by these stages the Mystic—who is rapt to the Beatific Vision by devotion—denotes the Path. In the Eastern world the Occultist—the Knower or Gnostic—sees the steps in somewhat other fashion, and divides the path into two great stages, the Probationary and the Path Proper; the Probationary represents the Purgation of the Mystic; the Path itself the Mystic's Illumination and Union. He further seeks to develop in himself on the Probationary Path certain definite "qualifications," fitting him to pass through the Portal which ends it; while on the Path itself he must wholly cast away ten "fetters" which hold him back from attaining Liberation or Final Salvation, and must pass through four other Portals or Initiations.

The qualifications must each be developed to some extent, though not completely, ere the first Portal can be passed. They are:

(1) *Discrimination:* the power to distinguish between the real and the unreal, the eternal and the fleeting—the piercing vision which sees the True and recognises the False under all disguises.

(2) *Dispassion* or *Desirelessness:* the rising above the wish to possess objects which give pleasure or to drive away objects which give pain, by utter mastery of the lower nature, and transcending of the personality.

(3) *The Six Endowments* or *Good Conduct:* control of the mind, control of the body—speech and actions—tolerance, endurance or cheerfulness, balance or one-pointedness, confidence.

(4) *Desire for Union,* or *Love.* These are the qualifications, the development of which is the preparation for the first Portal of Initiation. To these should the man address himself with resolution, who has made up his mind to travel forward swiftly, so that he may become a Helper of Humanity.

When he has acquired sufficient of these to so knock at the Door that it shall be opened unto him, he is ready to pass over its threshold and to tread the Path. He is initiated, or receives the "second birth." He is called among the Hindus the Wanderer (*Parivrajaka*), among the Buddhists "he who has entered the stream" (*Srotapanna* or *Sotapanna*); and before he can reach the second Initiation he must cast off wholly the "fetters" of: *Separateness*—he must realise that all selves are one; *Doubt*—he must know and not merely believe the great truths of Karma, Reincarnation and the Perfection to be reached by the treading of the Path; *Superstition*—the dependence on rites and ceremonies. These three fetters wholly cast off, the Initiate is ready for the second Portal, and becomes the Builder (*Kutichaka*) or "he who returns but once," (*Sakadagamin*); he must now develop the powers of the subtle bodies, that he may be useful in the three worlds, fitted for service. The passing through the third Portal makes him the United (*Hamsa,* "I am He"), or "he who does not return," save with his own consent (the *Anagamin*). For the fourth Gate should be passed in the same life, and for him who has passed that, compulsory rebirth is over. Now he must throw off the fetters of *Desire*—such rarefied desire as may be left in him—and of *Repulsion*—nothing must repel him, for in all he must see the Unity. This done, he passes through the fourth Portal, and becomes the Super-individual (*Paramahamsa,* "beyond the I") or "the Venerable" (*Arhat*). Five are the filmy fetters that yet hold him, and yet so hard is it to break their cobweb subtlety that seven lives are often used in treading the space that separates the Arhat from the Master, the Free, the Immortal, "He who has no more to learn" in this system, but may know what he will by turning on it his attention. The fetters are: desire for life in form, desire for life in formless worlds, pride—in the greatness of the task achieved, possibility of being disturbed by aught that may happen, illusion—the last film which can distort the Reality. When all these are cast away forever, then the triumphant Son of Man has finished His human course, and He has become "a Pillar in the Temple of my God who shall go out no more"; He is the Man made perfect, one of the First-born, an Elder Brother of our race.

XII

Our Elder Brothers

L et us now consider the relation to the world of Those who stand at that great height and who yet are of the human family, our Elder Brothers.

All religions look back to a founder who rose high above humanity; all ancient history tells of lofty Beings who laid the foundations of nations and guided them during their infancy and youth. We hear of divine Kings, of divine Dynasties, of divine Teachers; the testimony of the past is so unanimous, and the ruins remaining of past civilizations are so mighty, that we cannot reasonably declare the testimony to be worthless, nor the civilisations to be the unaided product of an infant humanity.

It is also noteworthy that the most ancient Scriptures are the noblest and most inspiring. The *Classic of Purity* of China, the *Upanishads* of India, the

Gathas—fragmentary as they are—of Persia, are far above the level of the later religious writings of the same countries; the ethics found in such ancient books are all authoritative, not hortative, they teach "as having authority and not as the scribes."

No religion denies or ignores these facts as regards its own Teachers and its own Scriptures; but, unhappily, most are apt to deny or ignore them where the Teachers and the Scriptures of other religions are concerned. Students of the *Wisdom* realize that all these claims must be impartially recognised or impartially rejected; and Occultists know that while many legends and fables may have gathered round these mighty Beings, nonetheless They, of a verity, have existed in the past and exist in the present.

The Occult Hierarchy which rules, teaches and guides the worlds is a graded Order, each rank having its own multifarious duties and carrying them out in perfect harmony, working out a portion of the plan of the Supreme Lord, the Logos of the system, in a service which "is perfect freedom." Two leading departments of our section of this Hierarchy are concerned, the one with the ruling, the other with the teaching of our worlds.

Those whom the Hindus call the four Kumaras* are the Chiefs of the Ruling Department, and the

---

*The *Bhagavad-Gita* (X, 6) refers to these as "The Ancient Four." H.P. Blavatsky says in reference to them: "Higher than the Four is only One."

Manus of Rounds and Races are their Lieutenants with, below them, the grade of Adepts, which numbers among its members those called Masters, to carry out the details of their work. Theirs is to guide evolution, to shape races, to guide them to continents builded for their dwelling, to administer the laws which cause the rise and fall of peoples, of empires, of civilisations.

At the head of the Teaching Department stands the "Enlightened," the Buddha who, when He passes away from earth, hands the Teacher's staff to him who is to become a Buddha in his turn, the Bodhisattva, the actual Teacher of the worlds. This Supreme Teacher is the ever-living Presence who overshadows and inspires the world's faiths, who founds them as they are needed for human guidance, and who, through His Helpers among the ranks of Adepts, guides each religion so far as is permitted by the stubbornness and ignorance of men. Every great spiritual wave flows from this department of the White Brotherhood, and irrigates our earth with the water of life.

In the grade of Adepts alluded to above are Those to whom the name of "Masters" more peculiarly belongs, in that they accept as chelas, or disciples, those who have reached a point of evolution fitting them to approach the Portal of Initiation, and are resolutely striving to develop in themselves the qualifications before described. There are many of this rank in the Hierarchy—those who have passed the fifth Initiation—who do not take pupils, but are engaged in other work for the helping of the world. Even beyond this rank some will still keep under their charge chelas who have long been devoted to them, the tie formed being too sacred and too strong to break.

The Theosophical Society is an open road whereby these great Teachers may be sought and found. We have amongst us those who know them face to face; and I, who write, add my humble testimony to that which has echoed down the ages, for I too have seen, and know.